The Makah

Sharlene and Ted Nelson

Franklin Watts
A Division of Scholastic Inc.
New York • Toronto • London • Auckland • Sydney
Mexico City • New Delhi • Hong Kong
Danbury, Connecticut

Note to readers: Definitions for words in **bold** can be found in the Glossary at the back of this book.

Photographs © 2003: Coast Guard Museum Northwest: 36; Davidson Gallery: 13; Makah Cultural and Research Center: 46, 47 (Janet Friedman), 25, 48 (Eric Long & Keely Parker), 18 (Makah Museum), 7 (Theresa Parker), 44, 50 (Keely Parker), 4 (Debbie Presten); National Geographic Image Collection/ Richard Schlecht: 12; nativestock.com/Marilyn "Angel" Wynn: 26; North Olympic Library System/Bert Kellog Collection: 43; Olympic National Park/Gunnar O. Fagerlund – #OLYM1542: 28; Pat O'Hara: 21; Penrose Library/Northwest and Whitman College Archives: 33; Ted Nelson: 51; Tom & Pat Leeson: 14, 24; MSCUA University of Washington Libraries/#NA1107: 40; Valerie Henschel: 8; Washington State Historical Society, Tacoma: 31 (Clallam Co), 3 bottom, 3 top, 16, 23 (Curtis), 34, 38, 41 (Morse), 30 (Museo de America, Madrid, Spain), 37 (James G. Swan).

Cover illustration by Gary Overacre based on a photo from MSCUA University of Washington Libraries #NA556.

Map by XNR Productions Inc.

Library of Congress Cataloging-in-Publication Data

Nelson, Sharlene P.
    The Makah / by Sharlene and Ted Nelson.
        p. cm. — (Watts library)
    Summary: Examines the history, culture, religious beliefs, poetry, and contemporary life of the Makah Indians of Washington State.
    Includes bibliographical references and index.
    ISBN 0-531-12168-2 (lib. bdg.)   0-531-16215-X (pbk.)
    1. Makah Indians—Juvenile literature. [1. Makah Indians. 2. Indians of North America—Washington (State)] I. Nelson, Ted W. II. Title. III. Series.
E99.M19N45 2003
979.7004'979—dc21
                                                2003000955

Contents

The Makah practice their seagoing skills in a whaling canoe.

A Whale Hunt

On a spring morning, seven Makah men paddled their cedar canoe across Neah Bay. The water was calm and reflected gray, drizzly clouds as the canoe rounded a point and headed west. Onward the men stroked, past rocky shores and along the forested cliffs of Cape Flattery.

When the canoe reached the Pacific Ocean, the men paddled south in search of gray whales. The men shouted when they saw a whale spout. They paddled hard and drew close. The whale swam near the surface and was nearly as long as the 35-foot (11-meter) canoe. A man in the bow of the canoe pushed a harpoon into the whale's shoulder. Then he threw out a line that was attached to the harpoon. Floats on the line prevented the whale from diving too deeply. The crew hurriedly paddled backwards.

The whale dove, its huge tail flying out of the water and barely missing the canoe. The harpoon line jerked tight. The canoe leaped forward and plowed through the sea as the whale towed it. When the whale surfaced again, the man in the bow threw another harpoon. Another man fired a shot, and the whale died.

The men were silent. Only sounds of a rising wind and waves slapping against the canoe could be heard as the whale hunters offered a Makah prayer. Then they raised their paddles and cheered. It was May 17, 1999. This was the first Makah whale hunt since 1913.

Whale hunting had been a sacred part of Makah culture for centuries. They used the whale's **blubber** and meat for food and their bones for tools. In the 1800s, however, European and American whalers killed thousands of gray whales for their oil. Hunting was stopped when the whales neared extinction. By the 1990s, the whale population had increased to more than twenty thousand. The Makah then received permission from the U.S. government and the International Whaling Commission to resume their whaling tradition.

On this May morning, 20 miles (32 kilometers) from Neah Bay, the whale hunters were not alone. A Makah support boat followed the canoe, and a boat with television reporters circled

The Gray Whale

The gray whale is a marine **mammal** that swims from Mexico to Alaska in the spring and returns in the fall. Gray whales weigh up to 40 tons and reach 50 feet (15 m) in length.

about. Noisy helicopters from Seattle television stations whirled above. A United States Coast Guard vessel plowed through the waves.

The U.S. Coast Guard was there to protect the whale hunters from protesters. Minutes after the whale was killed, a boat filled with protesters arrived. Using loud speakers, the protesters shouted angry words at the Makah. They wanted the whales saved, not hunted.

The hunters tied the whale's tail and the canoe to a Makah

Grateful for the whale, the Makah offer a prayer of thanks.

fishing boat for the tow to Neah Bay. As the boat rounded the point at dusk, it was raining. The men climbed back into the canoe to tow the whale to the beach. Canoes carrying members of five other northwest tribes joined them as they paddled toward shore.

Hundreds of people wearing raincoats and holding umbrellas gathered on the beach to greet the hunters. They cheered, whistled, and sang traditional Makah songs. Some beat a steady rhythm on drums. Horns honked. Farther out in the bay, the protesters blared an air horn. Then, like their ancestors, the Makah offered a prayer for the whale.

This photograph shows the rocks and gulls of Cape Flattery.

Chapter One

People of the Cape

The ancestors of today's Makah called themselves *Qwidicca-atx*, which means "People who live by the rocks and seagulls." The rocks are part of a massive headland that juts into the Pacific Ocean. The headland, now called Cape Flattery, is at the most northwesterly corner of the lower forty-eight states of the United States. The Makah have lived near the cape for four thousand years.

This remote corner is known for its harsh winters. Pacific storms lash the coast

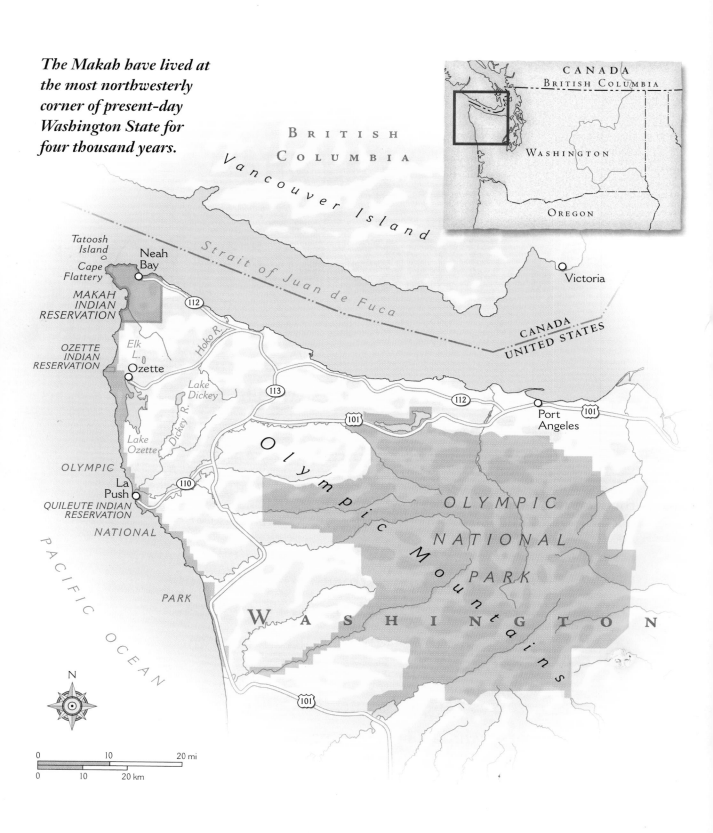

The Makah have lived at the most northwesterly corner of present-day Washington State for four thousand years.

CANADA
BRITISH COLUMBIA

WASHINGTON

OREGON

BRITISH COLUMBIA

Vancouver Island

Strait of Juan de Fuca

Victoria

CANADA
UNITED STATES

Tatoosh Island
Neah Bay
Cape Flattery
MAKAH INDIAN RESERVATION

112

OZETTE INDIAN RESERVATION

Elk L.

Ozette

Hoko R.

Lake Dickey

113

112

Port Angeles

101

101

Dickey R.

Lake Ozette

OLYMPIC

110

La Push
QUILEUTE INDIAN RESERVATION

NATIONAL

101

O l y m p i c

OLYMPIC

NATIONAL

PARK

PARK

M o u n t a i n s

W A S H I N G T O N

PACIFIC OCEAN

101

N

0   10   20 mi
0   10   20 km

with high winds and bring more than 100 inches (254 centimeters) of rain every year. Nourished by the rains, a thick forest spreads inland toward the slopes of the Olympic Mountains. Summers are cool, and fog often cloaks the coast.

Twenty miles (32 km) north of the cape, across the Strait of Juan de Fuca, lies Vancouver Island in British Columbia, Canada. A people known as Nootka, also called Nuu-chah-nulth, once lived on the island. The early Makah were closely related to these island people. They shared a language and a culture that was intertwined with the sea and the forest.

Villages by the Sea

The early Makah lived in five permanent villages. Di'ya, which later became known as Neah Bay, and Bahaada were located on the Strait of Juan de Fuca. Wy-atch, Tsoo-yess, and Ozette faced the Pacific Ocean. In each village, wooden longhouses stood above the beach. Close by a freshwater stream flowed from the forest to the sea. In Ozette, the largest village, there were fifteen longhouses.

Makah longhouses were up to 70 feet (21 m) long and 40 feet (12 m) wide. They were built with thick planks from western red cedar trees. Using **adzes** with sharp stone blades, heavy stone hammers called **mauls**, and wooden wedges, men split the planks from a tree's trunk. They lay the planks one above the other and tied them to supporting poles with **withes** of twisted cedar twigs to form the walls. Planks laid across pole rafters formed nearly flat roofs. There were no windows, but

11

Ozette was the largest Makah village.

Western Red Cedar Trees

Western red cedar, or cedar for short, is an evergreen tree with a soft, light-colored wood that splits and carves easily.

the roof planks could be moved to provide air vents. A doorway opened toward the sea.

Twenty to thirty people lived in a longhouse. Most were members of extended families. Each family had a fire pit for cooking and warmth. Cedar plank partitions provided some privacy. Cedar plank benches lined the walls. At night family members slept on the benches.

The most important person living in a longhouse was the chief. He was a whaler who had learned his whaling skills and

Several families lived in each longhouse.

inherited the title from his father. The chief and his immediate family occupied a large space in a back corner of the longhouse. Commoners, who were relatives of lower rank, lived in spaces along the walls. Slaves, people seized from other tribes or born from slaves, lived near the door.

Several chiefs lived in each village. No single chief ruled a village or the tribe. Instead, Makah life revolved around the families living in each longhouse. A chief's importance depended on his success as a whaler. His wealth depended on the skills of his longhouse family members in obtaining food and materials from the sea and forest.

The Sea

The sea provided the Makah with a rich harvest of food. In addition to whales, they hunted other marine mammals. Fur seals were hunted as they swam northward in the spring. Hair seals and sea lions were hunted in caves and on beaches.

Men caught halibut and cod over offshore reefs and fished for salmon in the ocean and in streams and rivers. The fishermen baited their hooks with tiny herring. Shore birds and sea birds added to the Makah diet. Women pried shellfish, such as mussels and barnacles, from shoreside rocks and dug clams from beach sands.

The sea was also a source of equipment and tools. Sealskins, inflated like balloons, made floats to help capture whales.

One Word, Two Meanings

In the Makah language, the word for food is also the word for fish.

Sea lions were among the marine mammals hunted by the Makah.

Long strands of dried seaweed were made into rope. Sharpened mussel shells were used as small knives and harpoon tips. Carved whalebones served as handles for cutting and carving tools. Empty clamshells became spoons and dippers. Small seashells were worn as decoration.

The Forest

The forest enabled the Makah to harvest food from the sea. Their big whaling canoes and smaller canoes for sealing and fishing were carved from cedar. Many of the canoes came from trees cut in the forest. Others were carved from logs tossed on the beach in winter storms. Strips of hard alder or maple protected the canoes' **gunwales** from the wear of cedar paddles.

The Ancient Forest

Cape Flattery's forest lies in a coastal forest belt known as a **temperate rain forest**. This name comes from the long, summer growing season and the abundant winter rains. Evergreen trees, such as western hemlock, western red cedar, and Sitka spruce, dominated the forest of the Makah's ancestors. These trees were among the biggest and the oldest in the world. Some reached heights of 200 feet (61 m) and grew to be nearly a thousand years old. Smaller evergreen yew trees and broad-leafed **deciduous** trees, such as alder, maple, and cherry, grew beneath the forest's giants. Ferns and salmonberry and huckleberry bushes carpeted the forest's floor.

Today, after nearly a century of logging, young trees dominate the forest of the Makah. Examples of the ancient forest of early Makah time can be seen in nearby Olympic National Park.

For centuries, the Makah carved canoes from cedar logs.

Whalers and sealers made harpoon shafts from the dense wood of yew trees. They bound mussel-shell tips to the shafts with cherry tree bark and smoothed the tips with pitch from spruce trees. Whalers made thick whaling ropes with cedar withes. Fishermen made lines with cedar bark and nets with cedar roots. Fishhooks were shaped from hemlock branches.

The Makah found many uses for cedar bark. Women pounded the bark to make it soft, then wove baby diapers, capes, and skirts. Working at upright looms, they wove warm blankets from strips of cedar bark, feathers, and wool. The wool came from dogs that the Makah raised for their soft fur. Shellfish were gathered in baskets loosely woven with cedar roots and limbs. Tightly woven baskets held food, tools, and utensils. People wore cedar bark hats for protection from the rain or the sun's glare.

The Makah hunted animals of the forest with yew bows and cedar arrows. The animals' sharpened bones made fishhooks and arrowheads. Elk antlers formed blades for **chisels** and the barbs behind harpoon tips. Elk and deer meat was served with seafood. Whalers wore bearskin coats. Beaver teeth became tools for cutting and carving as well as game pieces.

No Word for Shoes

In the ancient Makah language there was no word for shoes. The Makah were always barefoot.

The Makah expressed their spiritual beliefs in carvings.

Chapter Two

A Way of Life

The Makah way of life, their daily endeavors and their quest for food, was spiritually centered. They believed all plants and animals of the sea and forest had spirits. Over all these spirits there was one Great Spirit, the Creator of Daylight. The Makah sought spiritual helpers for guidance and protection. In dreams they found inspiration for songs. They expressed their beliefs in stories, ceremonies, and carvings.

The Spirit World

In thought, action, and prayer, the Makah showed reverence for the spiritual

The Legend of Thunderbird

Long ago, the Makah were very hungry. Thunderbird, a supernatural being, flew over the sea and captured a whale. He returned with it and saved the Makah from starvation.

The Salmon Cycle

Salmon are born in rivers and streams, and then they swim to the ocean. After several years, they return to their birthplace to deposit and fertilize their eggs.

life in all things. Before thrusting a harpoon into an animal or cutting into a cedar tree, they prayed to the Creator of Daylight. Each Makah asked to be worthy of taking creatures and plants for the food and materials upon which his or her life depended.

Whalers began uniting with the spirit world long before the whales' arrival. Again and again, they swam alone in secret pools. The whalers dove slowly, then rolled to the surface and blew water to imitate the whale's spout. By acting like the whales, they believed the whales would surrender to their harpoons.

On the day of a hunt, each whaler and his crew of seven men pushed their canoes from the beach. In the pre-dawn darkness they paddled to sea, guided by stars that were also a part of their spirit world. The whalers' wives remained in bed with their heads pointing away from the sea to encourage the whales to come quietly to shore. When the whalers returned with whales in tow, they were welcomed with chants, songs, and prayers to thank the whale for the things it would provide.

When two seal hunters approached fur seals sleeping among the ocean's swells, they remained quiet. Noise would startle the seals, and their spirits would be offended if the men pointed at them. Hair seals and sea lions were taken with heavy clubs. The clubs were carved with images of the animals as a sign of respect for their spirits.

The Makah spoke of the salmon as people who lived beneath the sea. Each year from spring through fall, the

Salmon-People swam to streams and rivers. The Makah greeted them as though they were chiefs of a great tribe. After the salmon were caught and cleaned, their bones were carefully placed in the water to ensure the salmon's return.

Makah carvers, working in wood and bone, connected the spirit world with items used in everyday life. Boxes, bowls, spoons, trays, tools, and combs carried images of sea life, animals, and birds. Other designs were symbols of spirits or beings seen in dreams and visions.

A salmon returns from the ocean to the freshwater.

21

A Forest Pharmacy

The Makah found many of their medicines in the forest. Fern tea cured coughs. Salmonberry bark numbed toothaches. Hemlock bark stopped bleeding.

Carvings on large cedar planks and posts showed the deeds of whalers and their encounters with supernatural beings. Ceremonial masks represented animals and beings such as Thunderbird and Wolf. The masks were painted in bold colors with red clay, ashes, or cherry bark roots mixed with salmon eggs.

Seasons by the Sea

As winter turned to spring, the Makah began stocking food for the next winter. Seas grew calmer, and fishermen in one-man canoes paddled daily to their favorite places to catch halibut and cod. Some families left by canoe to camp at temporary villages near the best fishing.

Beginning in the spring, Makah beaches were busy places. Men cut blubber from whales, and women cut blubber from seals. They melted oil from the blubber by placing it in canoes or boxes with water and fire-heated stones. They scooped the oil from the water and stored it in sea lions' stomachs for use as a dip to flavor food.

When fishermen returned with their fish-filled canoes, their catch was spread on the beach for cleaning. Some fish were eaten fresh. Most were prepared for winter use. Slices of halibut and cod were placed on longhouse roofs or hung like laundry on tall racks to dry in the sun. Salmon were smoked over wet-wood fires. Once dried or smoked, the fish were stored in baskets.

Elsewhere on the beach, boys and girls played a rough-

and-tumble game with sticks and a ball made of wood or whale **gristle**. They moved the ball through goals set far apart on the beach. Boys wrestled in the sand to improve their strength. Near shore, boys and girls paddled child-sized canoes to practice canoeing skills.

Along the beach, women continued their year-round gathering of shellfish. In the forest, they peeled strips of bark from cedar trees for weaving. Throughout spring and into late summer, they collected berries. The berries were eaten fresh or molded into small cakes for wintertime use. Other kinds of

For centuries, the Makah removed meat, blubber, and bone from whales in traditional ways.

The Makah still roast salmon in the traditional way.

plants and bark were collected for food or medicinal purposes.

Makah women prepared food using recipes handed from generation to generation. Some recipes were kept secret as part of a family's tradition. They roasted fresh fish and meat over fires on a framework of cedar sticks or wrapped the food in wet leaves to steam it over hot coals. Soups and stews of shellfish, meat, or dried fish were simmered in watertight cedar boxes. The boxes were filled partially with food and water then fire-heated stones were added for boiling or simmering. Fresh or dried berries added flavor.

When seas were calm, the Makah loaded containers of oil, dried fish, whale products, and items made from shells into their canoes and set off to trade with other tribes. To the south they traded for weaving materials or food not found in the sea and forest of the Makah. To the north they traded for large war canoes.

The Sea Warriors

During times of war, Northwest Coast tribes, including the Makah, traveled in war canoes to defend their territory, to take revenge for an unfair trade, or to capture slaves.

When winter winds blew and rain poured, the Makah gathered inside their fire-lit longhouses. Children listened to stories and legends told by their elders. Women wove baskets and blankets. Men prepared for another season of hunting and fishing. Carvers worked with their tools of sharpened stones, shells, bones, and beaver teeth. For fun, Makah men and women played games using shells, guessing games with colored wooden disks, and games of chance with dice made from beaver teeth.

Masks were an important part of Makah culture.

Ceremonies

Ceremonies were an important part of Makah life. They were held to keep order within the villages, to heal the sick, and to celebrate important events. At these ceremonies villagers performed dances, chants, and sacred songs.

The Wolf Society held secret ceremonies several times each winter. The society brought chiefs, commoners, and slaves together as equals. Those initiated into this society were bound together by specific rules and teachings.

Makah doctors held ceremonies to treat the seriously ill. Doctors were men or women who had gained special spiritual powers in visions or dreams. The

25

Sacred Songs

Sacred songs came from visions and dreams. Their short verses were sung in chantlike melodies accompanied by a rattle. Most songs were considered to be personal property. Only their owner could perform them. If the owner of the song died before passing it to a family member, the song also died.

Potlatches are an age-old custom among tribes of the Northwest Coast.

Makah believed that illnesses were not just physical but also could be caused by psychological or spiritual conditions. The ceremonies varied depending on the cause of the illness.

Potlatches were major ceremonies in Makah life. They were usually held by a wealthy chief to announce important events such as a marriage or the naming of his heir. The chief's longhouse families helped with the preparations. When all was ready, men paddled to distant villages to deliver invitations. Standing on a village beach, one man shouted out the day the potlatch would begin and the names of those invited.

When the guests arrived, some from as far away as Vancouver Island, they crowded into the chief's longhouse and were seated by rank. The chief spoke. Sacred songs were sung and danced. Stories were told. The guests listened and later would tell others what they had observed. This was how the Makah kept a record of important events in their lives.

To show his appreciation, the chief shared his food with the guests and gave them gifts of blankets, boxes, and furs. Some potlatches lasted two weeks. The chief knew that his generosity would be returned when he was invited to a potlatch.

A Makah made this rock carving when sailing ships first arrived.

Chapter Three

The Beginning of Change

English explorer Captain James Cook sailed past the Makah lands in 1778 and gave Cape Flattery its name. There is no record of contact between Cook and the Makah. To the north, however, Cook's sailors found the Nootka eager to trade sea otter **pelts** for bits of metal. The finely furred pelts were taken to China, where they sold for high prices.

When English and American traders learned about the profitable trade, they sailed to the Northwest Coast. They found all the coastal tribes eager to trade sea otter pelts for metal, tools, kettles, blankets, and trinkets. The traders' arrival marked the beginning of change for the Makah.

Houses on the Water

The Makah called the traders "house on the water people." One was English trader Captain John Meares. In 1788, Meares sailed close to Cape Flattery. "In a very short time we were surrounded by canoes," he wrote. Twenty to thirty Makah men in each canoe were wearing sea otter robes, and their faces were painted black and red. One of the Makah was Chief Tatoosh. This first encounter between the Makah and white men was brief. Meares was unable to find a place to anchor his ship. He named a small island near Cape Flattery after the chief and sailed away.

Chief Tatoosh wears a knobbed hat, which indicates his high rank.

In 1791, American Captain Robert Gray, sailing out of Boston, Massachusetts, came to trade with the Makah. Gray's fifth mate, seventeen-year-old John Boit, wrote, "Off a small Island called Tatoosh we collected many otter. Fine halibut and salmon were produced in abundance."

Sea otters were hunted to near extinction by the early 1800s. The

Makah saw few ships again until the 1840s. Then American whalers began coming to Neah Bay to obtain whale oil to add to the oil they had taken at sea. For the Makah, whaling had been a spiritual quest for food and material, but now it became a business.

Trade and Tragedy

Trade brought change. Makah fishermen became wealthier. Metal kettles replaced boxes for cooking. Nails replaced cedar withes for attaching longhouse planks. Buttons and shiny beads replaced seashell ornaments.

Trade also brought tragedy. Men aboard the ships carried diseases such as smallpox and measles. Coastal Indians had no

A Spanish Fort

The Spanish came to the Northwest Coast to claim new land. In 1792, they built and briefly occupied a small fort at Neah Bay.

This village was abandoned after an outbreak of smallpox.

immunity to the diseases, and many died. The Makah escaped this early spread of disease. Then, in 1852, a ship's crewman brought smallpox to the Makah. Probably one-third or more of the tribe died, and many of their sacred songs and family stories died with them. The village of Bahaada was abandoned as survivors moved to Neah Bay.

The Treaty

Washington became a United States territory in 1853. Issac Stevens, the territory's first governor, set out to **negotiate** treaties with all the tribes in his vast territory. Treaties were the government's way of making the tribes give up their lands to make room for white settlers. They were also a way of forcing the tribes to abandon their way of life, to become farmers, and to live like white people.

In January 1855, Governor Stevens sailed into Neah Bay. Makah people and some of the chiefs canoed out to meet with him aboard the ship. When farming was discussed, one chief said, "He wanted the sea. That was his country." Stevens saw that Makah life depended on whaling and fishing, and the dense forest was no place to farm. He said the government would send kettles for cooking blubber into oil, and "lines and implements to fish with."

In exchange for this promise, the Makah agreed to live on a **reservation**. The reservation of 27,000 acres (10,930 hectares) included forest land, Cape Flattery, and several miles

Reservations

Reservations were lands granted to the tribes by the U.S. government. Settlers could not live on reservations without tribal permission.

of beach along the Pacific Ocean and the Strait of Juan de Fuca. On January 31, 1855, the Makah signed a treaty with the U.S. government.

The Makah, especially the elders, did not trust the U.S. government.

Chapter Four

Life With the Agents

Little changed for the Makah immediately after the treaty of 1855. No settlers came to this remote corner of the territory. Travel was by boat, and the nearest town was 90 miles (145 km) away. Then, in 1861, Henry Webster, the first Indian agent arrived at Neah Bay to represent the U.S. government. Webster and the agents that followed came to oversee the lives of the Makah. The Makah, especially the elders, did not trust the agents. They believed the agents were sent to support the white peoples' interest and not those of the 624 members of the tribe.

Pitchforks to Fishhooks

The elders' worries about the government's intent came true when a ship dropped anchor in Neah Bay in 1862. It was supposed to bring the kettles and fishing implements promised by Governor Stevens. Instead, it brought hoes, pitchforks, and scythes for farming. The Makah men turned the scythes into blubber knives and made the pitchforks into fishhooks.

More worrisome were the agents that followed Webster who tried to stop potlatches. One agent said they were

After the agents arrived, the Makah held potlatches on Tatoosh Island where a lighthouse had been built in 1857.

wasteful. The Makah should save and not give things away. To avoid the agents, the Makah began holding potlatches on the beach at Tatoosh Island.

Another agent speaking for the U.S. government told the Makah that potlatches were illegal. The Makah continued to hold them, however. They told the agent that they were celebrating a birthday or having a Christmas party. This pleased the agent. He thought the Makah were beginning to adopt the ways of white society.

School Days

The first schoolteacher of the Makah was James Swan, who had visited Neah Bay in the late 1850s. He often ate with the Makah in their smoke-filled longhouses and dipped his dried halibut in whale oil. Although he was sympathetic to their ways, he felt Makah children should be given an education.

James Swan: Frontier Scientist

James Swan was born in Massachusetts in 1818 and traveled to the Pacific Northwest in 1852. After living among the Chinook Indians near the Columbia River, Swan came to Neah Bay. Always curious about Indian culture, Swan recorded facts and made sketches in journals. Later, he wrote a book about the Makah that was published by the Smithsonian Institution in 1870.

Under Webster's direction, Swan built a schoolhouse at Neah Bay. On opening day in 1863, only one student appeared. Swan had an idea. He showed the boy a **magic lantern**, an early version of a picture show. When other children learned about the magic lantern, they came to school. Swan knew the children liked to sing, and he composed a song to help them learn the alphabet. He let the girls weave baskets and taught the children how to collect fossils. Webster's boss, however, thought Swan was too patient and kind, and he was not effective in teaching white peoples' ways. Swan was dismissed in 1866.

Another teacher was assigned. The children continued attending school during the day, but at night returned to their longhouses and Makah ways. In 1874, a new agent established a boarding school to take the children out of their "surroundings and put them in the midst of a civilized Christian home." The school stood near the Indian agency buildings 2 miles (3.2 km) east of Neah Bay.

This photograph shows government buildings near Neah Bay, which included the agency headquarters and, later, a boarding school.

When village families were ordered to enroll their children in the boarding school, they protested. The agent threatened them and put one father in jail. With no other choice, parents placed their children in school. Some moved to Neah Bay to be near them.

Wearing shoes and cloth clothes, the children lived at the school ten to twelve months each year. In class they were told that Makah ways were evil. They were allowed to speak only in English. The teacher taught lessons from the Bible. Before meals, the children recited a Bible verse. On Sundays, they attended church services conducted by the agent.

New Ways

The government's agents could make Makah children attend school, but they could not make their fathers become farmers. Instead, the Makah found new ways to harvest crops from the sea. Whalers continued to trade whale oil, but by the 1870s the sealskin trade had become more important. Rich people in Asia wanted sealskin coats. Rich Europeans wanted sealskin hats.

Profits from hunting fur seals were so high that some Makah bought their own sailing schooners. Makah women served on board as cooks and helped to skin the seals. White men were hired to work aboard the vessels. Some Makah sealers loaded canoes on their ships and sailed to Alaska's Bering Sea to hunt. In 1890, an observer said that the Makah "all have plenty of money; far more than if they attempted to make a living by farming. . . ."

A Makah Named Lighthouse Jack

Lighthouse Jack earned money carrying goods to the lighthouse on Tatoosh Island. With canoes lashed together, he delivered firewood, cows, and furniture.

When the price paid for sealskins went down and the government tried to stop the overhunting of seals, Makah men turned to halibut fishing. The competition with other halibut fishermen was fierce. Hundreds of small boats crowded the harbor at Neah Bay. In 1898, the agent reported that the Makah halibut catch reached 10,000 pounds (4,500 kilograms) per day. The fish were sold to fish-processing firms and canneries.

Along with their seagoing businesses, the Makah continued taking whales, seals, and fish for their food. When not weaving baskets, the women gathered shellfish and berries. Steamships came each week to Neah Bay. They brought canned goods, bags of flour, sugar, and salt, which the Makah used with their seafood and berries.

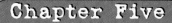
A Future With a Past

At the beginning of the 1900s, only a few Makah still lived in the outlying villages of Ozette, Tsoo-yess, and Wy-atch. Neah Bay had become the tribal center. By then the Makah had been under the rule of government agents for nearly forty years. During that time, they had proven to be a resourceful people. They were far better off than most of the tribes who had signed treaties in 1855.

Still, the agents had brought change. Healing ceremonies and the Wolf

Society had been banned. Potlatches were still held, but in the disguise of parties. Slavery had been abolished, and warfare with other tribes had stopped. English had become the younger generation's preferred language.

A Village Changed

In Neah Bay the longhouses were gone. In their place, wood-frame houses stood on streets along the beach. Single families occupied most houses. The boarding school had been abandoned, and some children attended a day school. Other Makah children were sent to distant boarding schools. There was a hotel owned by a Makah, and there was a store owned by a white man named Wilbur Washburn. On one street corner stood a Presbyterian Church established by a missionary named Helen Clark.

Competition from non-Indian fishermen had made halibut fishing less profitable. Makah men worked as loggers when companies began harvesting timber on reservation lands. Traveling by boat or canoe, others found jobs elsewhere. Men worked in canneries and saw mills along the Strait of Juan de Fuca. Families picked summertime crops on inland farms.

The agent continued to encourage farming, and Makah women grew vegetables in small gardens. They also used their basket-making skills. Some sold baskets on street corners in the city of Seattle. Others traded baskets at the Washburn store. A small basket bought a loaf of bread, and a larger basket bought a pair of shoes.

Helen Clark, Missionary

Helen Clark came to Neah Bay in 1898 and stayed for twenty-five years. Her sermons were given in English and then translated into Makah.

In 1900, these children attended a day school that had replaced the boarding school.

New Freedoms

In 1924, the U.S. government granted American citizenship to the nation's Indians. The Makah wanted to celebrate and began a new tradition. They held their first Makah Day with ceremonial singing and dancing in the streets of Neah Bay.

By then, the village at Ozette had been abandoned. A wagon road connected Neah Bay's streets to the villages of Wy-atch and Tsoo-yess. In 1931, a state highway connected Neah Bay with the outside world. For the first time, the Makah could travel to distant places by car instead of by canoe or boat. Tourists and sport fishers could drive to Neah

Makah children became interested in learning traditional ways.

Bay. A year later, the agency school closed and a public school was built.

The Makah gained their greatest freedom when Congress passed the Indian Reorganization Act of 1934. Under the act, the Makah began to regain some control of their lives and lands. They signed the Makah Constitution and elected a five-member tribal council as their government.

After the last agent left, the Makah no longer had to disguise potlatches as Christmas parties. Some of the customs and secret societies eventually faded away, but other customs continued to thrive. Now the Makah were free to renew their old customs.

Young people began to show an interest in the Makah past. When Makah Day approached, children, men, and women rehearsed dances to perform at the celebration. In the 1960s, elders visited the schools to teach Makah words and to share basket-weaving and carving skills with the children. Except for stories and legends, however, there was little evidence of the ancient Makah's lives. Then, their past became linked to the present by a winter storm that raged over Cape Flattery.

A Link to the Past

In February 1970, huge waves washed against a mud bank at Ozette. The waves exposed an old canoe paddle, fishhooks, and pieces of cedar boxes. The Makah called Richard D. Daugherty, an **archaeologist** from Washington State University at Pullman, Washington. Daugherty drove to the coast and hiked to the site with members of the tribal council. They were excited. They thought the **artifacts** might come from a longhouse lying beneath an ancient mud slide.

Daugherty set up a camp at the site. His team built cabins with wood that had washed up on the beach. Food, shovels, water pumps, and hoses were brought in by helicopter. Archaeologists, college students, and Makah began slowly hosing away the mud. They found whalebones, longhouse planks with carved images, sleeping benches, looms for

Archaeologists

Archaeologists study remains and artifacts to learn about human activities of the past.

45

Archaeologists work at uncovering artifacts at the site in Ozette.

weaving, and a box holding a blanket. Carved wooden bowls still smelled of seal oil.

Daugherty concluded that the mud slide had occurred about five hundred years ago. It suddenly had buried several longhouses while villagers were going about their daily lives. The gooey mud had kept the artifacts from rotting. **Excavation** work continued for eleven years. More than fifty thousand artifacts were recovered. Each piece was cataloged and taken by helicopter to Neah Bay for cleaning, preserving, and display.

The Ozette discoveries revealed new information about the ancient Makah. Archaeologists learned of their use of looms for weaving blankets. The carved objects showed great skill and a highly developed form of art. More importantly, the Makah could see and touch the things that they had only heard about in legends and stories.

Removing artifacts at Ozette was back-breaking work.

Sealing and whaling canoes are displayed at the museum at the Makah Cultural and Research Center.

Chapter Six

The Makah Today

Today, visitors from around the world come to see the Makah artifacts uncovered at Ozette. They are displayed in a museum at the Makah Cultural and Research Center in the small town of Neah Bay. Along with the artifacts, there are full-sized models of a longhouse and seagoing canoes.

Keeping the Culture Alive

At the cultural center, the Makah study the artifacts for more clues to the past.

Makah Days feature traditional songs and dances performed by children.

Elders translate old stories into English. Children and adults learn to read, write, and speak Makah. Carvers and weavers work with wood and bark from special cedar trees reserved in the Makah forest.

Makah Days are held every August. The three-day festival is a reminder of the celebration first held when the Makah received their citizenship in 1924. There are songs, masked dances, and canoe races. Salmon, roasted over fires in the traditional way, is shared with hundreds of visitors.

The Makah may hunt whales today as they did in 1999. People against the hunts have tried to stop them in federal courts, but judges have ruled that whale hunting is a Makah right. When hunting, the Makah use their traditional ways. As required by the International Whaling Commission, however, a high-powered rifle will be used for a humane kill, and a motorized vessel will tow the whale toward shore.

A Makah cleans the raceways where young salmon are raised at the fish hatchery near Neah Bay.

Government and Enterprise

Today there are 2,300 Makah tribal members. Half live in Neah Bay, while others live off the reservation. Many young Makah go away to college and return to Neah Bay to work at the cultural center, in schools, at a health center, and at the headquarters of the tribal government. Like all Neah Bay residents, they shop at the modern Washburn store that was established a century ago.

The tribal government employs two hundred people and oversees programs for the benefit of the tribe. With the U.S. National Marine Fisheries Service, the Makah operate a fish hatchery on the Sooes River. Makah foresters harvest

51

trees and plant seedlings on the reservation forest. Makah dock their commercial salmon fishing boats at a new marina built by the tribe. The tribe harvests spiny sea urchins, sea animals whose meat is desired in Japan. Makah scientists are studying the use of ocean waves to generate electricity.

Visiting the Cape

Besides visiting the cultural center and enjoying Makah Days, visitors can hike a trail to the edge of Cape Flattery and look across to Tatoosh Island. Except for the lighthouse, which still guides ships, the island is little changed since Captain Cook sailed by in 1778.

Near the cape, visitors walk sandy beaches where Makah women still collect shellfish. To the south, in Olympic National Park, a trail leads to the site of the Ozette village where the Makah linked their past with the present.

Timeline

1778	English explorer Captain James Cook sails along the Northwest Coast and names Cape Flattery. Sea otter pelts obtained from a tribe on today's Vancouver Island are later sold in China for a great profit.
1788	In search of sea otter pelts, English captain John Meares makes the first recorded contact with the Makah. He names Tatoosh Island for a Makah chief.
1791	American Robert Gray obtains sea otter pelts from the Makah.
1792	The Spanish build and briefly occupy a small fort at Neah Bay.
1815	The trade in sea otter pelts is all but ended after the animals are hunted to near extinction.
1840s	American whalers begin sailing to Neah Bay to obtain whale oil from the Makah. The trade lasts only a few years.
1852	Nearly one-third of the Makah die of smallpox.
1853	Washington becomes a U.S. territory.
1855	The Makah sign a treaty with Territorial Governor Issac Stevens. The tribe retains 27,000 acres (10,930 ha) of land and the right to continue fishing and hunting whales and seals.
1857	The U.S. government builds a lighthouse on Tatoosh Island.
1861	The first of many U.S. Indian agents arrive in Neah Bay to oversee the Makah.
1863	James Swan opens the first Makah school in Neah Bay.
1869	The business of hunting fur seals and selling their skins begins. Profits help the Makah for nearly three decades.

1874	The Indian agent establishes a boarding school 2 miles (3.2 km) east of Neah Bay. All Makah children are required to attend.
1880	Halibut fishing begins as an important Makah business that lasts for several decades.
1898	Helen Clark, a missionary, arrives in Neah Bay and later establishes a Presbyterian church.
1913	Gray whales are near extinction, and the Makah hold their last traditional whale hunt.
1917	The few families at Ozette abandon their village and move to Neah Bay.
1924	The Makah and other American Indians are granted U.S. citizenship. In celebration, the Makah hold their first Makah Day.
1931	A state highway is completed to Neah Bay. It is the first road connecting the Makah with the outside world.
1932	The first public school opens in Neah Bay.
1934	Congress passes the Indian Reorganization Act, a law allowing American Indian tribes to choose whether or not they want to be self-governing.
1936	The Makah decide to be self-governing, and a tribal constitution is signed.
1970	Ancient longhouses and their contents are discovered at Ozette and excavation begins.
1979	The Makah Cultural and Research Center is opened. Artifacts from Ozette are displayed at the center's museum.
1981	Excavation at Ozette is ended after more than fifty thousand artifacts are recovered. A Makah fish hatchery begins operation.
1999	The Makah kill a gray whale in a revival of their whale hunting tradition.

Glossary

adze—a tool for cutting and carving wood

archaeologist—a scientist who studies ancient people by digging into places where they lived

artifact—an object made and used by people in the past

blubber—the fat of whales and seals

chisel—a tool with a cutting edge to shape wood or stone

deciduous—a tree that loses its leaves before winter

excavation—exposing objects by digging

gristle—tough, fiberlike material in meat

gunwale—the top edge of the side of a canoe or boat

immunity—protection from a disease

magic lantern—an early method to show pictures using a projector and transparent slides

mammal—a warm-blooded animal whose young drink their mother's milk

maul—a heavy hammer

negotiate—to reach an agreement through discussion

pelt—the skin of a dead, fur-bearing animal

potlatch—a ceremony where the host provides a feast for guests and gives them many gifts

reservation—land set aside for a special purpose

temperate rain forest—a forest with a long summer growing season and abundant winter rains

withes—a slender, flexible branch or twig

To Find Out More

Books

Beck, Mary Giraudo. *Potlatch: Native American Ceremony and Myth on Northwest Coast.* Portland, OR: Graphic Arts Center Publishing Company, 1993.

Blashfield, Jean F. *Washington.* Danbury, CT: Children's Press, 2001.

Eder, Jeanne M. Ogawin. *The Makah.* Chatham, New Jersey: Raintree/Steck-Vaughn, 2002.

Hobbs, Will. *Ghost Canoe.* New York: William Morrow and Company, 1997.

Sullivan, Robert. *A Whale Hunt.* New York: Scribner, 2000.

Organizations and Online Sites

The Makah Tribe
P.O. Box 115
Neah Bay, WA 98357
http://www.makah.com/
This is the official site for the Makah.

The National Museum of the American Indian
http://www.nmai.si.edu
Part of the Smithsonian Institution, this museum is dedicated to helping people learn about Native American cultures.

University of Washington Libraries Digital Collections
http://content.lib.washington.edu/aipnw/renker/
This site presents historical essays about the Makah.

Makah Cultural and Research Center
Bayview Avenue, Highway 112
P. O. Box 160
Neah Bay, WA 98357
http://www.makah.com/museum
This site gives information about the cultural center and the museum.

A Note on Sources

We first became acquainted with the Makah in 1970, when we read articles in Seattle newspapers about the artifacts being found at Ozette. Years later, we loaded our backpacks and hiked to the old village. By then, remnants of the excavation were covered with wild shrubs and berry bushes, but we could see where the longhouses once stood. We walked the beach where whaling and sealing canoes had been brought ashore for centuries. We climbed over rocks where Makah women once gathered shellfish.

After a drizzly night at Ozette, we drove to Neah Bay to visit the Makah Cultural and Research Center. At the center's museum we saw the Ozette artifacts and stepped inside a replica of a longhouse. Then we hiked Cape Flattery to see Tatoosh Island. A few years later, we hiked to Ozette with our two grandchildren, and we told them the story of the people who once lived there. Little did we know that someday we would write about the Makah.

When given the opportunity to write this book, we began by researching the written records. We started at the Library of Congress in Washington, D.C. Closer to home, we did research at the archives at the Washington State Historical Society, the University of Washington, Seattle's Museum of History and Industry, Seattle's public library, county libraries, and online sites. These sources yielded information from books, journals, government reports, magazines, and newspapers.

Then we again visited the Makah Cultural and Research Center. We talked with Janine Bowechop, the center's executive director. Janine is a Makah and a graduate of Dartmouth University. We listened to elder Helma Swan Ward, who was translating Makah stories into English. Helma's maiden name, Swan, came from pioneer James Swan. One of her grandparents asked Swan if they could adopt his name, and he agreed. In the museum, we shared Makah history with Kirk Wachendorf, the museum's interpretive specialist.

We would like to thank the people at the Makah Cultural and Research Center whose help made this book possible. They are Janine Bowechop and those on her staff, including Maria Parker Pascua, Kirk Wachendorf, Helma Swan Ward, and archivists Keely Parker and Theresa Parker.

—*Sharlene and Ted Nelson*

Index

Numbers in *italics* indicate illustrations.

About the Authors

Sharlene and Ted Nelson have written many books based on years of shared experiences. They attended the University of California at Berkeley and were married after graduation. As Ted pursued a career in forestry, Sharlene became a freelance writer while raising their two children.

Having lived on the California and Oregon coasts, they wrote guidebooks to West Coast lighthouses. Their first book for Franklin Watts, about logging in the old west, was inspired by their years living in a remote logging camp.

While sailing on the Columbia River in May 1980, they watched Mount St. Helens erupt. This led to a Children's Press book about the eruption. Hiking in national parks inspired three more books for Children's Press.

The Nelsons' home overlooks Washington's Puget Sound and the Olympic Mountains.